From Wear to Wye

*To Suzanne
with my love
Fi
xx*

From Wear to Wye

Fi Benson

Douglas McLean Publishing

Coleford, Gloucestershire

Published by
Douglas McLean
8 St John Street
Coleford
Gloucestershire
England
GL16 8AR
© Fi Benson 2009

This book is sold subject to the condition that it shall not, by way of trade or otherwise, be lent, re-sold, hired out or otherwise circulated without our prior consent in any form of binding or cover, other than that in which it is published and without a similar condition including this condition being imposed on the subsequent purchaser.
British Library Cataloguing in Publication Data
A CIP catalogue record of this book is available from the British Library

ISBN 978-0-946252-72-5

Printed and Bound in England by
Cpod, A division of The Cromwell Press Group, Trowbridge, Wiltshire

Introduction

Fi Benson lives in the Forest of Dean, Gloucestershire but travels regularly between the Forest and her original home town of Sunderland, Tyne and Wear – both physically, and 'in her head'.

She is a freelance writer, primarily a poet and playwright. Two of her full-length plays and a number of sketches have been performed by the Everyman Theatre, Cheltenham. Her work has been performed in rehearsed readings in the Carriageworks, Leeds. She was commissioned by Show of Strength Theatre, Bristol/Everyman Theatre to devise a touring piece of platform theatre for the Brunel bi-centenary. She has been involved in several community performance projects locally.

In 2008, Soundworks and the Forest Bookshop, Coleford initiated a programme of monthly cabarets to be held at the Garden Café, Lydbrook as part of the Coleford Festival of Words. Fi began taking part in the cabarets from December, as the 'Lydbrook Scribe.'

The sketches that follow are presented as they were spoken, and are not intended as perfectly written prose.

Notes:
1. In *From Mireystock to Highnam: Me and Radio 3*, the radio presenter's dialogue is an approximation rather than the actual words spoken, due to the roadwork condi-

tions in which Fi jotted them down. Fi hopes she will be forgiven for the coconut comment.

2. Adult Games was written partly as a tribute to the playful nature of the cabarets which often included interactivities such as those mentioned at the end of the sketch.

Table of Contents

From Mireystock to Highnam 9

Janus and the Butterflies 19

Like Riding A Bike 31

The Chapel of Garioch 49

Adult Games 59

Me and Eddie 65

From Wear to Wye 73

From Mireystock to Highnam

Performed at the Garden Café & Gallery
December 2008

I'm climbing into the car at not quite the crack of dawn but definitely among the splinters. I'm away up the lane through Camomile Green, left down Worral Hill, on past the narrow ribbon of the river Lyd and I'm heading for the Mireystock crossroads.

I haven't turned the radio on yet, it's quiet in the car, just me catching my breath between the domestic landscape and the travelling one, just me indulging in an overture of anticipatory silence.

It's early to be leaving the village, the cottage, the study that's my writing room, but today's one of those days when I turn back into an academic to go and do college work in Cheltenham, so one of those days when I have to engage with the A40 and its major roadworks, please expect delays.

I'm turning left at Mireystock, and … am I sitting comfortably, then let the radio begin …

Tune in to Breakfast for a more elegant way to start the day, presented during the week by Rob Cowan or Sara Mohr-Pietsch

... more peach, more plum, less banana. I always imagine Ms More-Peach to have long strawberry-blonde hair, pink cheeks and soft fleshy features when in fact she's angular, with short dark spiky hair, Sara 'More-Coconut' rather than 'More-Peach'.

I'm passing the quarry with the yawning ravine that looks like a great place to play cowboys and Indians or today's PC equivalent. It'd make a great place for an ambush. I see warrior-braves with their bows and arrows standing tall on top of the jutting stone, I see the sheriff and his deputy and the entire posse riding along the cycle path.

You wouldn't think a cornet would be an instrument of virtuosity but it is when it's played by Bruce Dicks.

Or is that Dickey? I miss the surname while I try and avoid smacking into the back of a Fiesta that has chosen to brake suddenly in front of me for no apparent reason.

I listen to Dickey's cornet as I pass the Brierley Swan and watch a perfect and elongated V of geese fly over the Forest. The symmetry of the geese's synchronised formations is breathtaking. It's a particularly sunny September, balmy, soft.

I bet they're tempted not to go, let's just stay here. Travel can be hell, full of delays and irritations, let's not bother.

I avoid slipping into thoughts of the potential road chaos that I'm likely heading into and tune my mind back into Radio 3.

Next is the Blue Danube by Strauss, written in response to a military defeat that Strauss was particularly sad about.

I'm passing the little island of shops with the crazy coloured lettering, passing the Cinderford lights, driving up the winding hill past the church, in reverse slalom towards the summit of the Plump.

I'm greeting the Gorgon tree.

Morning, lovely morning, how're ya hanging?

The Gorgon, with its long, wild and straggly branches is one of a special collection. The collection that's called My Favourite Trees. These include the old bearded-man tree at Speculation, the Truncated-trunk Elephant tree at Sallow Vallets, the Gorgon tree just before the summit of the Plump.

And now an aria. In the royal palace the captive princess regards her fate ...

In the green Laguna the me regards the sharp bend.

Up and over the top of Plump Hill, with that tricky contortion that involves an irresistible glancing over to the right to view the horseshoe-bend of the river Severn – while simultaneously turning the car to the left, trying not to slither over the middle white line into somebody else's lane. Oh, sorry, mate, lovely view.

Then down, down the other side into Mitcheldean, past The Old Smithy Stores that had that great reserve Shiraz once, and past The Lamb yet another pub that's closed to become a bed and breakfast, and on towards the mini-roundabout and that risk of the mini-roundabout conundrum.

Give way to the vehicle on your right. But if there are vehicles at each approach, nobody can move, everybody's trapped in a perpetual circle of Highway Code courtesy. After you, after you, after you, after you. What the hell, after me.

Beeeeeeeeep!

Well, somebody has to move, we can't just sit here all day. Places to go, things to do, Radio 3 to listen to …

Locatelli's Introduttione No 5 in D.

Crusell's Romanze, Clarinet Quartet No 1 in E flat.

Mompou's Canción y Danza No 3.

I have absolutely no idea what all these figures mean, but they spin me round in an alpha-numeric kaleidoscope of musical nomenclature.

Bach's Fantasia & Unfinished Fugue in C Minor.

The very sounds of the titles, their phrasings and rhythms, are music to the ear.

Palestrina's Chanticleer.

Chanticleer! The name given to the cockerel in the Nun's Priest's Tale, tale of many apostrophes and also the Chaucer choice while I was at St Thomas Aquinas Secondary School, just down the road from Hylton Castle where I had my first sexual fumblings.

Chanticleer. God I loved English. Kes. Antony and Cleopatra. Tess of the D'Urbervilles.

Oi you tit!

A white van man, Business Express, cuts me up in the middle of a suicidal overtake on a blind bend. *His* suicidal overtake.

Dickhead!

Ave Maria Grazia Plena. Celebrating the spiritual, the medieval, the Italian. Sit back and enjoy.

And I do, through Longhope, Little London and Huntley.

Next we have a baritone singing Borodin. We are having a lot of bass this morning.

And now James Macmillan with 'A New Song'.

This is the title of the piece - A New Song. Jimmy clearly doesn't get the whole naming thing. No numbers, no flats, no major-minors, or minor-majors. It's just *A Song*, and it's *New*.

And now the Breakfast News at 7.30

Shares have fallen sharply across Asia.
Rebel MPs rally against Gordon Brown.
Sanctions against Zimbabwe remain.
Damien Hirst raises 70 million pounds at Sotheby's.
America plans an increase of troops into Afghanistan.

One of my own girl-babies has grown herself into a red-capped lance-corporal, on the UK's Afghan list for next year. Underneath the raspberry beret she's a designer-girl with a shoe fetish. I can imagine her spending a lot of time trying to shove the yellow stilettos into the kit bag.

Onward, onward, to the front line, of the A40, I am approaching the Highnam roundabout.

From Mireystock to Highnam

I can smell cornflakes, mebbe they're harvesting cereals in a nearby field. By a strange co-incidence there's a van in front that's declaring Gibbons as the family loaf, but I've little time to reflect that as a family we've never eaten a Gibbons loaf, before Savage Plumbing noses its way in between us.

Gibbons and Savage, me and a lane full of other vehicles, crawl so slowly along the A40 we could be part of a leisurely theatrical promenade. If only the performance we're attending weren't so damned dull. The seemingly unhurried ploddings, stationary poses, of a fleet of dirty mustard vehicles and their crews.

And now the weather. Temperatures are high for this time of year, and there may be the possibility of light showers in the south west before the end of the morning.

Well, we left the sunshine behind in Churcham. It's heaving down, there is no sky, just a sky-sized opening in the top of the world where the water's falling through. Or maybe a lake that's only just realised it can't fly and is rushing back down to earth before it's missed.

I'm passing the spot where last July somebody's blue Volkswagen floated merrily up the dual carriageway.

And I'm watching the rain fall.

And I'm thinking of the Great Gloucestershire Floods of 2007.

We're all watching the rain fall.

Next a bit of Gallic subtlety, Fauré's Romance, with Gil Shaham on the violin and Akira Eguchi on the piano. Composed apparently to the accompaniment of grinding teeth because Fauré's family found his working process laboriously slow.

Police Speed Check Area 30 mph.

You could knock the nought off, cos we're barely doing three, creeping forward wheel-turn by wheel-turn by wheel-turn ...

Over Farm, The Toby Carvery, the Wharfside Restaurant. Businesses Open As Usual.

No, you can't just turn in, please drive to the furthest roundabout you can see, negotiate it as best you can considering it's chocker with other traffic and has are-they-working-are-they-not traffic lights every six feet, and then drive back the other way, yes, that's right, the way you've just come.

No, it is not businesses open as usual.

Variations on a Hungarian Air, Hurlstone.

Strauss' Introduction to a final scene, Moonlight Music.

Copland's Midsummer Nocturne.

Borodin's Polovtsian Dances, from Prince Igor.

From Mireystock to Highnam

Foulds' April-England.

Lumbye's Champagne Galop.

Outside of the car, it isn't Hungary, it's not midsummer or April, and there is no moonlight.

Outside, there's no prince and absolutely no champagne, galloping or otherwise.

But inside the car, thanks to Radio 3, I have all those things.

This is Sara Mohr-Pietsch, and with the clock telling me that it's nearly four minutes to eight, it's time to bring on the Trolls.

Janus and the Butterflies

Performed at the Garden Café & Gallery
January 2009

It's been said of writing, 'Writing's easy, all you do is stare at a blank sheet of paper, until drops of blood appear on your forehead.'

It can be intense.

So, during a writing day, I'm often taken with an urge to be out somewhere, but with no desire to join the real world just yet.

I've found the perfect palliative for this condition – Cannop Ponds.

It's far enough away from me cottage to provide a change of backdrop, but not that far away that I have to expend vast amounts of fuel getting there, me carbon footprint already size seven or thereabouts …

And Cannop's generally not too peopled. People tend to belong to the real world, and can be very distracting if you happen to be an extrovert with an automatic interaction reflex.

Hi there!
Afternoon.

Ah, what a cute baby.

What d'ya call your dog?

Another advantage of the ponds is that, not only does it provide me with plenty of space to walk – because it's true, I am a walker – but its criss-cross of paths, fairly flat and relatively Roman-road straight, is easy-peasy terrain that I don't have to think about, that doesn't demand any of me attention, that just is.

Which brings me to the subject of my tale …

The second of January, 2009

I find myself parking-up at the entrance to Cannop Ponds. This is a lie of course, cos to *find* yourself means that you've had to lose yourself, and I haven't, because I've just driven here deliberately. But what I *have* found is a new reason for being right here, right now, at the start of the year.

And it's this …

The living moment is everything.

D H Lawrence

The moment is the only thing that counts.

Jean Cocteau.

You must live in the present, launch yourself on every wave, find your eternity in each moment.

Thoreau at Thinkexist.com

I do believe in that wisdom, that life is all about *the moment*. But this is New Year, which is all about the future, wall to wall with resolutions ...

And on top of that, there's the fact that I have a huge alter ego as a list person.

Not meaning that I lean to one side, though I clearly do have leanings, but talking about the obsessive compulsive behaviour that sees me at every solstice, birthday, anniversary, or Wednesday, making copious notes of what I want to have done, and where I want to have been, in five years' time, next year, next month, next week, tomorrow ...

It's really hard to delight in the miracle of the moment, when you devise spreadsheets for your resolutions, and you've been writing SMART objectives since you were eleven.

Aware of my listing activities, people often say to me admiringly *'aren't* you organised.'

No, I'm not.

I'm just chasing butterflies ...

Because as far back as I can remember, I've wanted to live in the now, to savour every minute.

But it didn't take me long to come to the conclusion that I had in fact been born of a butterfly – that psychologically, biologically, and astrologically, I'm designed to flutter here, flutter there, flutter every flipping where ... that a moment is a really long time to stay in one place, or to hold on to a single thought.

Being in a state of perpetual transience, all whimsical and ephemeral, doesn't give you many opportunities to stop and savour.

And I've wanted to be a writer since ... well, eleven, and I thought, 'What sort of writer can't capture thoughts, and keep them still long enough to show them to somebody else? Not one that gets read or listened to.

That's when I realised I needed to net myself once in a while, or I risked disappearing up my own whimsy.

And that's when I started writing lists, in an attempt to pin myself down, and give myself a writing chance.

Back to the second January, the New Year, which is always a dangerous time for the list addict, and, remember, I'm a heavy user. So heavy recently that I overdosed.

For weeks, no netting, no pinning down of butterflies ... no completing of any written work ... unless you count the lists.

I've got a theatre director interested in my half-drafted play. I've got a publisher interested in my half-drafted novel. I don't want to waste those opportunities. Something has to be done!

But I'm in a quandary. I don't want to kick the list habit, because it's been valuable for years, I just need to shove it out of the way a bit.

On the other hand, I know that if I give the butterfly free rein I'll be a-flittering and a-fluttering, from now until next winter, going everywhere, but getting nowhere.

So on the second January I'm reviewing the situation, and full of Lawrence and Cocteau and Thoreau, I'm in Cannop, trying to concentrate on the now, not the butterfly nanosecond now, but the longer savoury now.

I give it a real go.

Everything's alright for a while.

From the entrance on the Speech House Hill, I stroll towards the ponds along the bumpity-bump lane, resisting the list-maker's temptation to count the speed humps as I step over them ...

I start, at the scuffle and dart of the squirrels ...

I smile, at the nest-protection strategies of the blackbirds - Ooo, somebody's coming, let's make lots of noise and launch ourselves like ground-to-air missiles. Look at us, leaving home, the nests are down there in case you were going to miss them ...

I listen to the breeze softly rifling through what leaves are left on the little tree, that's frozen into a pool of ice, just over the sheep-fence.

I watch finches flying to and fro, carefully selecting seeds on and around the small wooden tables erected by the RSPB.

I dwell on the sextuplet of swan children, that are not quite, not quite, totally-white of feather, and are still with their parents, all of them floating gracefully across a stretch of unfrozen water in the largest of the ponds.

Yes, it's going terribly well.

Maybe my lepidoptera are hibernating.

Maybe the list-maker is having a duvet day.

And, feeling warm fingers of sunshine on my skin, I am smug with the savoury now-ness of it all.

Briefly.

And then I'm thinking, aye, but there's summat missing, a lot of summat.

I reach the gate that marks the end of the picnic site and the beginning of the path that leads to Cannop Wharf.

Then I'm through the gate ... and into a completely different atmosphere.

Everything changes on the other side of that gate. The sound is more muffled. The light's more muted. Visual images appear slightly blurred; lines of demarcation are less distinct.

The contrast between before and after that gate is so stark I could have stepped into a different dimension.

And maybe I have.

Because I feel the tentative flutter of a butterfly's wings, not that deeply inside.

I set off up the narrow path.

My butterfly awakens, and I do absolutely nothing to stop it, even though I know I'm going to be seduced by myriads of images that will dissolve shortly after contact with my brain, that will disappear like seed-heads in the wind.

My butterfly flitters ...

Underneath the surface of the ice on that pond, silver-white wings spread wider and wider. The ice-siren opens her mouth to sing, loud and sweet, and her crystal feathers tremble with pleasure. The warmth of her pleasure melts the ice above her.

Inside that old and broken tree there are ten turquoise spiders, spinning webs that interweave between the prongs of a pearl and emerald crown ...

The way into the kingdom of the knife sprites lies in the gap between those two boulders, and is guarded day and night by twenty-one boxes, not cardboard, but creatures that are half bat — half fox ...

Those layers of frozen fungus at the base of the wooden post are rows of seats in an elves' auditorium ...

The screech that just rent the air is the call of the daystallion, cousin to the nightmare ...

I've reached the signposts at the cross-paths beside the Wharf. There are people ahead, so I take the turn towards Dilke Bridge.

To my left the landscape is dark and gothic, dense with tall evergreens. To my right the forest opens out, filled with brushwood and ferns and fallen ivy.

My butterfly flutters …

Those flecks of ice are the tears of a giantess who passed this way at dawn, searching for the son who was stolen in the night.

Among those blades of grass, are clumps of hair, torn out in a tantrum, by Geliel, one of the twenty-eight angels who govern the mansions of the moon.

I happen to glance into the brushwood side of the path, as a wren alights on a branch close by.

Almost immediately it's joined by a second wren.

The birds are next to each other, but facing in opposite directions.

They call to mind Janus, the god of January, and gateways, and beginnings and endings. The god with two faces, looking at the past and the future at the same time. Clever!

I'm thinking of Janus, and I'm wondering about the joiny bit up the middle of his heads, when I realise that he's standing right next to me.

Just like the marshmallow man in Ghostbusters, think of him and he appears, whether you want him there or not.

I have no green slime at my disposal.

Butterflies are one thing, I've lived with the butterflies forever, but Janus is new, and he's walking by my side.

Which is a bit weird …

... so I, very politely, turn my head to one side, the side where Janus isn't.

As I do so, I glance over into the gothic side of the path, and see that I'm parallel with a long passage through the trees ending in a series of archways – none of which I can say I've ever noticed before.

Now, you'll realise I'm a frequent visitor to Cannop, and I'd say I'm fairly familiar with all of its pathways, so the passage comes as a surprise.

But maybe it's not surprising that I haven't seen the passage, maybe it's only ever here during very certain conditions, at exactly this point in the winter, during exactly this type of weather – and it has been unusually cold?

Or maybe it's never existed before, right here, right now, just for today

And likely there aren't any archways; it's just the formation of the trees, viewed from this particular angle, creating an illusion.

Still, they remind me of something. I've stood in front of archways shaped exactly like this before.

Ah, the painting. The White Doe of Rylstone, which is depicted wandering through ruins, with a series of archways behind it.

A second later, Alice Through the Looking Glass, *I'm* through the painted arches, and I'm standing in Leeds City Art Gallery.

The air's hot and sticky, just like it was last summer when I first saw the painting.

Well, paintings, actually.

Because there're two others that I loved.

I know where I want to go next.

I walk through the exhibition rooms, and here the paintings still are.

Well, why wouldn't they be? If this is last summer.

I stand and admire the Grimshaws. Not an elderly couple, sharing cheese and tomato sandwiches and a pot of earl grey tea, but

Snow and Mist, Caprice in Yellow Minor, painted by John Atkinson Grimshaw in 1872

and his *Tree Shadows on the Park Wall,* 1892.

Each painting contains a solitary figure, who is walking away into a distance where the lines of demarcation aren't quite distinct, where the landscape is slightly blurred … a landscape of trees in the one painting, and snow and mist in the other.

The figures could be different people, or they could be the same person but in different settings …

I recall that I wanted to write their tale, but the butterfly was restless.

With this thought, the paintings dissolve, like chalk drawings on a pavement in the rain ... The painted archways disappear ... and I'm standing on the path that leads between the Cannop Wharf and the Dilke Bridge.

I see that Janus hasn't gone anywhere, and doesn't show any signs of doing so, so I set off back down the path.

And I start to chat – probably the interaction reflex kicking in ... but actually what I tell him is the tale that I'd wanted to weave for the solitary figures, an epic tale of mistaken identities, disastrous journeys and overturned prophecies.

I'm so preoccupied with the story, that me and Janus have passed the Wharf, crossed the picnic site and reached the end of the bumpety-bump lane before I realise it.

I open the car door to let the odd god in ... and it's only then that I notice he has butterflies in his hair.

Settling into the passenger seat, he hands a scrap of paper to me to read. Hell's teeth, it's not a list is it?

It's this:

The present was an egg laid by the past and with the future in its shell. Zola Thurston

I realise, that although I don't understand the full of it yet, my writing's just turned an important corner.

Janus doesn't leave until I've finished writing up the tale, until the finish is smooth and polished.

I post my precious manuscript out to several eager editors on the first March.
But do I?
Because today's only the thirteenth of January, so how do I know?
Maybe it's an item on a list.
Or maybe I'm hatching an egg with the future in its shell.

Like Riding a Bike

Performed at the Garden Café & Gallery
February 2009

When I first come to live in the Forest I do what most people do in a new landscape, I set about exploring it. As soon as I've admired the Dean's more flagrant gifts – like Beechenhurst picnic site and the view from the top of New Fancy – I embark on a quest to unearth its hidden treasures, to unlock its secrets.

Who isn't compelled by secrets?

While I'm in the woods, unearthing and unlocking, I'm enchanted to discover a scattered population of half-pint wooden signposts. The half-pints bear bold arrows, directing me … straight up to the skies above … or diagonally towards the treetops.

To my continuing and bitter disappointment, I cannot fly, I can't even levitate though I have tried, nor can I climb fifty-foot trees. All of which means that I can't take advantage of the half-pints and their trying-to-be-helpful pointers.

When I later discover that the signs are intended for clusters of cyclists following the threads of a vast web of cycle tracks, I still can't take advantage, because one of the other things I can't do is ride a bike.

* * *

When my dad was a boy, he went out on his bike one day with a bunch of his mates. They went down to the sea-front where apparently they weren't supposed to go, my dad had a bad accident and he nearly died.

When my mam first told us this tale, to explain why me and my two sisters couldn't have bikes, I vaguely imagined there to be testicles involved.

Like when me, my sisters and my cousins used to garage-hop across the roofs of a row of garages behind my Auntie Lilian's in Hylton Red-House. Cousin Robert fell onto the railings behind the garages. He had a bad accident and he nearly died. Testicles were involved.

As for my dad's experience, it seemed insensitive to ask my mam for any further details. But many years later I learned that there'd been a collision in which the boy-father was thrown several feet in the air, landing badly, smashing his head against the ground.

Anyway, that collision was it for him and bikes, and consequently there were never any cycles for us girls. While the rest of the neighbourhood's kids, our friends at school, everybody else in the entire known universe, had them, *we* didn't. They just weren't allowed.

By extension of the cycle-wheel prohibition we weren't even allowed roller skates, but my mam bought us them anyway and we practised with them whenever my dad wasn't around.

I always felt extremely adventurous, strapping those roller skates on to my feet, even though I would wait to do so until I was beside the front gate so that I could hang on to the garden wall while I practised.

I'd gingerly sidestep-roll-sidestep-roll from the gate to where our bit of the wall ended and Mrs Marshall's started. Then I'd repeat the performance. Down, then back, down, then back, over and over again.

There was a slight incline to the pavement outside our house in Lichfield Road which made the wheels roll ever so slightly quicker than I was comfortable with. But I made sure the wheels weren't overly oiled which helped to slow me down just enough to stay in a relative-comfort zone.

Bit by tiny bit I felt safer and more courageous on those wheels.

Until one Sunday after dinner I was completely free of the wall, and although it was only down a length of about nine feet, I was *roller-skating*, properly roller-skating!

Three cheers for me! Queen of the rollers. Empress of the skates. A bold adventurer, a lionheart.

At that very moment, my dad came round the corner of the street, himself rolling, back from Fulwell working men's club, a darn sight more oiled than my skates had ever been.

I wondered if there might be trouble, if I should call the cavalry who were just then at ease in the sitting room watching an old black-and-white film.

But from my dad's gestures and spasmodic mutterings, I gathered that he was quite impressed with my skating prowess.

Try from a bit further up, he encouraged.

Where he was pointing was only a few feet away, but territory can be minutely localised, and I realised that he was indicating beyond the boundaries of my skating sovereignty. And there was no handy wall.

But it's my dad! I was keen to rise to where his estimation of me was floating.

'Go on' he said, 'you'll be fine. I'll catch you if you fall.'

Okay ...

I teetered over to the new starting line, my tiny supply of confidence depleting by the teeter.

I stopped, I turned, I started to roll forward towards my dad ... but *I* wasn't setting my speed, the incline was.

So almost immediately it was ...

'Catch me, Dad ...'

But he wasn't quick enough, he missed my flailing hands. I hit the pavement, falling badly, smashing my head against the ground.

Funnily enough, the head banging puts me off freewheeling. I hang up my skates, my sceptre and my broken crown.

I might have spent the rest of forever licking my wounds but it isn't long before my royal status returns, when me and my sister Viv discover ... The Quarries.

Up the back of our road is a broken track that leads to a perimeter fence that me and our Viv climb through one Saturday afternoon, and find a whole new empire.

The Quarries are disused, and known locally as the Old Tip. They are a massive landscape of what me and Viv know is volcanic ash, left over from some ancient eruption and not yet cooled for the ground beneath our feet is still warm.

We know that an entire civilization is buried underneath.

And *we* are the regal guardians of this vast volcanic territory of slate and steel, pewter and silver, myriad shades of grey. Those are dotted here and there with brilliances. Green, blue and red, slivers of what might look to anyone else like old bottles and tin cans, but which we know are precious stones that have survived the fires and so possess powerful properties. They are emeralds, sapphires and rubies that we use as talismans against the Ash Bandits who lie all around us, merged into the upper crust, cleverly camouflaged so that their violent attacks are always by surprise.

To no avail. For me and Viv are Quarrior Queens, Ash Amazonians, and we are up to the fight.

With my life full of bandits and precious gems, I certainly don't have time to mourn the loss of a set of wheels.

Many years pass before what goes around comes back around.

***

When I first come to live in the Forest I'm twenty-nine with one nine-year-old daughter.

Abracadabra, I'm thirty-nine ...

... and izzy wizzy let's get busy, I have a further trio of children and for a decade, me and the quartet have been playing happily in the woods, paddling in the puddles, picnicking in the ferns.

But raising my head above the busy-ness one day, I spy the hosts of families out cycling together. It looks like jolly good fun.

And I spy solitary bikers, too, speeding hither and thither. It looks like flying, air beneath the bikers' wings.

Around this same time, me and the quartet often go at weekends to the Rising Sun at Moseley Green, a family pub with a play-park, toys in the pool room, a pond full of fish and frogspawn.

And sometimes kids on their bikes, Evil Knievel-ing off the edge of the surrounding woods into the car park.

And, increasingly it seems to me, bands of grown-up cyclists. All chatting and laughing and looking like they're having a hell of a time. I feel a bubbling resentment that I can never join in with this camarade community.

Leaving the pub, after their lasagnes and lemonades, the cyclists set off down the long drive to the main road. Some of them all Lycra-d up, self-contained and sleek, a shoal of fish heading for the sea. But others with their baggy teeshirts fluttering like feathers in a breeze created by their own flight ... fast and wild and free.

I watch the bikers.

I watch my children watching the bikers.

I realise that there's a cycle I haven't thought about.

Because we had no access to bikes, me and my siblings didn't learn to ride, but my children don't have access to bikes, and they aren't learning either. So it's completely possible that my children's children won't learn. And their children's children. A vicious cycle. I might accidentally be responsible for perpetuating a legacy of bike-less-ness through generations to come.

I'm all the more horrified because of my choice of mothering styles.

Early on, I have spurned that view of successful motherhood where the protagonist is cast in the leading role as house-keeper. Instead I've based my maternal behaviours on the philosophy that it's my job to help the children grow into independent adults, not assuming limitations down upon themselves, developing whatever it is they need to develop to find and follow their personal dreams, whichever path might lead to them ...

... not excluding cycle tracks.

In effect, by excluding the children from the joys of cycling I feel like I'm not doing my job.

And those family rides do look like tremendous fun ...

At the point I'm talking about the eldest is nineteen and pursuing a nineteen-year-old's pursuits. Although I don't know it, she's already learned to ride, while playing with Kim who lives up the Bourtts off Worral Hill. I'm totally unaware of this acquired skill, because while I'm busy with the trio of other children down in Camomile Green, the land above the Bourtts is out of eyesight and out of earshot, and might as well be the land of the giant at the top of the beanstalk. It wouldn't have come as a surprise if she'd returned from her play with a karaoke harp and a chicken that laid its own nuggets.

The trio have no Kim to assist them. They're close together in age and form their own small crowd of self-supplied companions to each other. None of these companions has a bike to say to another of them 'here have a go'.

Time for me to put a spoke in the wheel of our bike-lessness.

The trio need to learn how to ride.

I need to learn how to ride.

First problem of course is that I don't have a bike. So my girlfriend Kay offers to lend me hers.

She lives in a flat behind the old Co-op in Yorkley, and keeps the bike in her spare bedroom.

I drive over to Yorkley and wait in the courtyard behind the flats for her to fetch the bike.

Like Riding A Bike

I happen to be standing beside a row of garages – uncannily similar to the ones in Hylton Red House.

I'm a little unnerved.

Her flat is on the first floor, so she has to carry the bike across her shoulders down an outside metal staircase.

I watch the bike's approach.

She has a twenty-gear Raleigh Amazon. While I'm liking the sound of Amazon, I'm not liking the bike, which is large.

I start to feel a little clammy.

There you go she says, standing the Amazon next to me.

It has grown larger from the staircase to me.

And I've grown smaller.

And clammier.

Hop on, she says merrily.

If only.

The Amazon has a 'man's frame', and a ludicrously high saddle that I can't possibly reach if I want my feet to still touch the ground. And I do want my feet to still touch the ground.

I sort of flatten the bike sideways and semi-straddle the frame, but then am at a loss as how to get it upright and balanced with me on it.

So I get off.

I stare blankly at Kay.

You'll be fine she says, which I have heard before of course, but maybe she knows something that I don't, which of course she does, because she knows how to ride a bike.

Whilst I'm not predisposed to bow to her superior knowledge, I do give it a nod by going through the getting-on process a second time. The process is the same so the result is the same.

I get off and stare blankly at Kay.

You just need to get on and push off straight away, in one smooth movement. It's the motion that keeps it balanced, she instructs, still merrily.

I'm not prepared for composite skills; one at a time's going to be hellish enough.

I absorb my inadequacy, in silent despair.

Kay explains more about how the bike works, about gears in handle bars and alternating hands.

I can't possibly take any of this in, but perhaps her chattering has more to do with trying to lifting a shield of words against my silence, which has become so heavy that it's making stones fall down from the sky.

The stones smash against the courtyard. Shards of rock break off and ricochet against the garage walls and all around me.

I stare into the eye of the storm, and the eye stares back. Then it winks!

The clouds of despair retreat, the sun comes out and dries up all the stones, and I have an epiphany.

I need a littler bike.

A couple of weeks later I own one.

Like Riding A Bike

A family in Joyford Hill has advertised it in the *Review*, and now it's mine. It's a girl's bike, with five simple gears. It's purple and dotted with sparkling silver stars. I just thank god that it doesn't have Barbie stickers.

With further help from the *Review* the trio have bikes 'n all.

I buy a multi-pronged carrier from Halfords, fit it to the car, and we let the learning begin.

We engage in two modes of delivery.

One is the family session.

We park at Kay's flat then, because Yorkley Hill naturally has an incline, we walk the bikes down the Hill until we reach the entrance to the wide trackway that leads from Yorkley to Mallards Pike.

Across this entrance is one of the Forestry Commission poles that prevent cars driving through. Beyond the pole the track is relatively flat for about a hundred yards or so before climbing uphill. This flat track is the family training ground.

A pattern soon evolves.

Kay goes ahead with the nine-year-old twins who are succeeding, albeit haltingly, to ride, while she supports, reassures, prompts.

Me and the seven-year-old take up the rear, and make like the Baron von Drais.

In 1817, Baron von Drais from Mannheim invented a walking machine to help him get around his gardens faster. Effectively a bicycle without the pedals, he propelled himself forward by pushing his feet against the ground, rolling himself onward in a sort of gliding walk.

It's in Draisine fashion that me and my littlest boy traverse the track.

The training goes on for several weeks.

The twins are doing nicely thanks to Kay.

My Draisienne partner absorbs his inadequacies in a silent despair that is so heavy it makes stones fall from the sky. He is only seven so his stones are still pebbles, but as I watch the shards of pebble ricochet off the ground, I feel for his pain. I try and help with a little extrinsic motivation. The boy's a chocoholic. I tell him that if he learns to ride before I do, he gets a Black Forest gateau.

The very next session he succeeds, but we may never know whether it's because of the chocolate cake or because of a fall off his bike which so enrages him that sheer annoyance drives him to take control of that bike and just damn well ride! Strangely, a fall where testicles were involved.

No matter, it's three cheers for the children.

Hurrah, hurrah, they can all ride!

Which leaves me as the only member of the family who can't.

Although the day is warm and sunny, I pushbike – as in literally push-the-bike – through a veil of purple rain dotted with sparkling silver stars …

Throughout these family sessions, a sense of parental decorum has meant that I just about hold on to my emotions, just about manage to rein in my intense frustration.

Keeping it all simmering nicely until the grown-ups alone sessions ... when the same etiquettes don't apply ...

Careful reconnoitring of the Forest track-ways, worthy of warfare with an Ash Bandit, has resulted in my establishing just where me and Kay can go where there's a broad, flattish track and where I have seen no other cyclists go.

This absence might be due to the track consisting of an arc that leads only from one bit of New Fancy road to another, hardly inspiring to anyone other than an almost forty-year-old with a incline-phobia learning how to ride a bike. But the lack of onlookers makes it ideal for me.

A pattern soon evolves.

At the beginning of the arc, I straddle my bike, one foot on the ground.

Kay makes helpful suggestions, like 'I'll hold on to the back and push.'

I give her a look that says no, she won't.

The look says further that I don't appreciate her fussing and farting around, that it's no good her offering me any physical assistance whatsoever because I have to learn to do it by myself. That is the point. Her role is simply to distract attention away from my inactivity in case people come along, and to be the first to congratulate me when I ultimately succeed.

It's a long look, at the end of which Kay responds with an understanding that I find extremely irritating.

'I'll just leave you to it then' she says, before gliding off in an unnecessarily elegant and overly proficient manner, which I take as a personal slight.

I shrug off her insensitivity and carry on with my attempts to have both feet on the pedals at the same time.

Periodically Kay returns to insult me by asking if I'm alright and how am I doing? The air turns deep purple and silver-star-sparkly as I respond with words that rhyme with truck and trucking. Then off she goes again.

The training goes on for several weeks. During which I put so much intensity into what must look from the outside like somebody standing with a bike, that my clothes become drenched with sweat and my fingers end up so stiff and gnarled from death-gripping onto the handlebars that on one occasion Kay has to turn the ignition key for me to be able to drive home.

On the arc, in periods of blessed respite from the intensities, I drift into reverie ... about mastery of the wheel ...

... about the celestial cherubim.

That foursome of special angels who have direct access to God. Each having four faces – of a human, a lion, an ox, and an eagle. Each having four wings, and each having a wheel. The entire bodies of the quaternity – including their wings and their wheels – being full of eyes all around, in front and behind.

As each cherub rises up on their wings, so also do their wheels rise with them.

God's own unicyclists.

Everything alright? says a voice that I vaguely recognise as Kay's.

Yes of course. Why wouldn't it be? I'm only learning how to ride a bike for god's sake. It's not rocket science.

Ah good, she says, wheeling back along the arc.

Why can't I do it!

I'm a grown-up, a long way from childhood and Lichfield Road.

It's all Amy's fault of course.

Amy-g-dala.

Okay, I know it's pronounced Amlgdala, but Amygdala is also a comic-book villain in the Batman stories. Anyway, I prefer my pronunciation.

Amy is the almond-shaped nerve cells in the brain that control emotional associations. Encoding every emotion and physical sensation that we experience into implicit memories.

Implicit in that we aren't conscious of them. They're not written into our minds but into our flesh. For the vast majority of them, we don't know they're there.

Amy is mature at birth, active while we are still in the womb. Since a baby is created from its parents' cells ... doesn't that mean that our bodies inherit a legacy of secrets?

Who isn't compelled by secrets?

My head hurts ... maybe it's fallen off a bike.

I listen to my blood coursing through my veins, my heart pumping ...

Another epiphany.

I'm going about this bike learning business all wrong! I'm trying to control what I do using my mind ... when it's all in the flesh ... !

Maybe I can deceive the flesh ... I can't bike ... but I can dance.

What if I make like I'm dancing? The body might be filled with happy thoughts and stop fighting me.

I put my hands out to the handlebars as though I'm taking a partner.

I strike up the music, by singing to myself.

And I step out ...

I do it!

It might only last for eight revolutions, but I'm riding the damn bike.

I pour jolly cycling sensations into my cellular memory by joining sequences of eight revolutions together to go and show Kay how clever I am. Look, I shout along the arc, look what I can do.

Like Riding A Bike

Uni-cycling cherubim appear and line the track, clapping and cheering.

* * *

A week later, it's August Bank Holiday Saturday.

I've celebrated my success by buying a brand new bike – a burnt orange Silver Fox – from the cycle shop opposite The Swan in Lydney.

I'm out with the family, riding the Silver Fox from Yorkley Hill to Mallards Pike.

I am still a novice – I can't let go of the bars to make hand signals, I can only do corners if they're wide and spacious, and I don't do cattle grids at all ... but I am cycling and enjoying that longed for family ride.

As we join the track that leads around the Mallards Pike lake, I am charmed to see a wedding party on the path up ahead. Bride in a stunning ivory dress, bridegroom in coal black tails, bevy of bridesmaids in blood-red taffeta.

The charm fades away when I realise I'm going to have to employ what for me are advanced cycling skills in order to manoeuvre around the wedding party.

Several thousand cells begin to shout and scream, and I fear for the unsuspecting party, for the ivory dress.

But suddenly the bridesmaids' proximity to the lake reminds me of a story I once wrote ...

... about a bunch of flower-girls, whose spirits lived at the bottom of a lake.

As I approach the party I see the flower girls climbing out of the water, and grasping the hands of the bridesmaids. They are mischievous spirits. I suspect that they might want to pull the bridesmaids into the lake with them, but no, they only want to dance. So while the flower girls dance with the bridesmaids, I manoeuvre with preoccupied ease, and pass them all by, smoothly and safely ...

My family, who've ridden on ahead, only now dare to turn and see if all has gone well.

Without thinking about it, I lift a hand off a handlebar to give the thumbs-up.

To the sound of the family's rapturous applause, I catch a glimpse of celestial eyes winking at me from the treetops and the skies above.

The Chapel of Garioch

Performed at the Garden Café & Gallery
April 2009

This is one of the ways in which my tale might start.

I am predisposed to be interested in the spiritual and the supernatural because of two significant influences in my childhood.

The first was being raised as a Roman Catholic, living my daily life, taking my daily bread, among a paranormal population that included a God a Devil and a Holy Ghost. Where risings from the dead, and incidences of magic along a continuum of tiny to epic miracles, were as commonplace as toast.

The second influence was Hammer Horror, whose films I'd stay up and watch with my dad, late into Friday nights. Silent screams, dripping evil, houses that bled to death. God, they were great, I loved them.

During my adulthood, I've analysed and intellectualised, explored and experimented, all processes serving only to deepen, and broaden, my beliefs in the unseen. I've developed my own version of spiritual practice, I'll go into anybody's church, and because I really like the thought of them, with all their suggested intimacy and ancientness, I'm particularly drawn to chapels.

This is one of the ways in which my tale might start.

The Chapel of Garioch is not in itself a singular construction. It's a village that has lain for thousands of years in a parish which is also called the Chapel of Garioch. The village lies at a road junction near the banks of the river Don in Aberdeenshire. The parish is ten miles long from north to south, two – five miles from east to west, and forms an irregular figure. The irregular figure embraces the mansion-house and surrounding estate of Fetternear, where a crofter family called Davie lived and farmed from before the 1700s, and where many of them died and were buried, in a graveyard on the estate.

This is one of the ways in which my tale might start.

In the year of the new millennium, catalysed by our nana and then dad dropping their mortal coils, my little sister Diane starts to research the family history. Having more than a touch of the OCD it's not long at all before she's become an expert and has mapped the maternal-family back to the 17th century. Our mam, Anne Marie Davie, was born in Sunderland and so was my granda Frank. Beyond that, an ancestral string of Davies farmed in Fetternear, in the Chapel of Garioch.

The Chapel of Garioch

It's difficult, isn't it, to define the absolute beginning of any story. Because there are always so many different places to start, each of them the effect of something that's gone before it, or happened alongside of it. Threads in life's tapestry interweave, wefting and warping in chain-stitch reactions.

But a tale-teller has to start somewhere, that's the point of telling a tale, choosing where to pick up, and then to leave, one particular thread or another.

So ... this is the start of my tale.

It's 2005. After a series of geographical decisions, I've settled in the Forest of Dean. I've acquired a custom of staying for a few days now and then with my mam, back in Sunderland, so that we can indulge in quality one-to-one time. This year I say 'do you fancy going away somewhere, mam?' My mam says yes, she does, she fancies somewhere meaningful, what about the Chapel of Garioch, she suggests, the ancestral home of the Davies?

I only have to hear the word chapel to like the idea and am well up for it.

We consult with genealogist genie Diane to establish more specific details for our travel-plan. Diane likes the idea of the trip and she's up for it as well.

My eldest daughter Melanie happens to be in the northeast at the time, hears of the plan, likes the idea and she's up for it 'n all.

We are now a three-generational pilgrimage, setting out to walk the walk of the ancients. Be where they've been. Breathe where they've breathed. Boldly go where none of us living Davies have been before, to find the burial ground, say hi, how're you doing?

The night before the trip we all gather and sleep over at my mam's. We rise before dawn so that we can get through the Tyne Tunnel before the traffic builds up.

So, we're tired, right …

Diane's graciously offered to drive, which puts her in the driving seat. Our mam is our mam, so she's front passenger. Me and Mel are in the back … where neither of us normally are.

The journey to Aberdeen is a six-hour nightmare. Turning the normal bright and breezy, light and easy me into a bundle of petty irritations. As we approach Aberdeen and I learn that it's known as the Granite City I'm in empathy because I'm equally cold and crystalline.

I'm not the only one. By the time we arrive at the hotel relations are strained. But, after a scene in reception which is marvellously therapeutic, we come to our senses and make peace. It's as a united team that we dump our baggage in our rooms and set off out of the hotel and into the Aberdeen afternoon. It is a beautiful May Day; we have spring in our steps.

We're walking up the High Street, chatting merrily, when our Diane suddenly disappears across the road. We follow her into what turns out to be St Nicholas church and churchyard.

The grounds are beautiful and full of flowering cherry trees, whose petals are scattering like pink confetti in the warm breeze.

The pilgrim party scatters likewise, the whole dissolving into its individual parts, with their individual responses to the surroundings.

My mam finds a sunlit bench and parks to people-watch.

Our Diane, headstone-hunter, is already off stalking prey.

For Mel, it's let the photos begin, as she manoeuvres into studied shots of my mam against a background of floribunda.

I meself turn back into a writer with a taste for the surreal. I de-pocket a pocketbook and start scribbling ...

... a tale about the residents of those two graves with lids variably askew, both residents members of the undead fraternity who've arrived back at different moments from a night of vampiric frolics, neither of them yet aware of the other's existence, or the fact that they are twins separated at birth ...

... a story about what looks like intermingled moss and ivy covering that walled tomb, but which is really a sequence of veils discarded by Batna, one of the daughters of Lilith, and jilted on her wedding day by Lucifer's cousin, twice-removed

... a poem about the angel who has climbed down from her stone, stepped lightly across the path in front of me and is now polishing a tiny grave with her hair.

A shriek splits the sky in two.

It's our Diane.

I leave my mysticals behind as I hurry to Diane's side. She's found one of us, an Alexander. To find a dead Davie so soon in our trip, so unexpectedly in the high street, knocks me emotions further off-kilter and I'm gripped by a strong urge to shout out 'Grandad, we love you Grandad' and slobber grand-daughterly kisses all over the grave.

I fear that I'm becoming a little overwrought. I'd better acquire a modicum of calm before my encounter with a whole cluster of clanship at Fetternear.

The next days are packed solid with further familial adventures as we follow the ancients all around Aberdeen and the adjoining towns and villages.

We reach the final day and the culmination of our quest, to find the resting ground of our crofting ancestors. Because the pilgrimage so far has been a series of intense psycho-emotional journeys for all four of us, I fear we're looking a bit dug up ourselves.

The only directions to the graveyard that we've managed to amass are a road map with so few markings on it the nearer it gets to Fetternear that the graves could well be suspended across a black hole in space, and some handwritten lines, discovered in the family history office and which I've accidentally left back at the hotel. We are heading into uncharted territory.

By a miracle, we find the entrance to the Fetternear estate, and drive in, straight past the sign that says 'Private. Keep Out'. Not one of us demurs, we've journeyed far too far to be stopped by a daft little sign.

Some modern housing gives way to fields as we travel deeper and deeper into the estate. Eventually, the road peters out beside a sprawl of abandoned farm buildings and we have to stop. We park up next to one of the outbuildings and wonder where to go next.

While we're wondering, a battered red car appears out of nowhere, and a woman in wellies gets out and approaches us. We assume she's come to tell us to get off the estate. My mam adopts poor little old lady mode, explains why we're here and asks the woman if she knows the way to the graveyard.

'Oh, I'm just making a delivery,' says the woman, 'the people inside'll be able to tell you.'

We four look dubiously at the abandoned buildings.

'Squatters?' our Diane suggests

Wellie woman disappears into the dereliction, and reappears with a very friendly lady, who does indeed offer us some verbal directions to our graveyard.

But my mam's legs are too bad, and Mel's Italian leather shoes are too good for what is sounding like unpredictable terrain, especially as it's starting to rain. So my mam and Mel choose to stay in the car.

'Take lots of photos,' they shout after me and Diane as we set off, across a nearby footbridge and through pastureland where there are many more signs telling us to keep out …

Hours later we still haven't found the cemetery, even though we've walked to the other end of the estate and back again.

We are on the verge of giving up, when I see what I think might be a headstone sticking out of the grass. It's not, it's just a rock, but from its new vantage point, we see the remains of a stone archway, next to the ruins of a medieval church, behind which we finally discover the burial ground of our ancestors.

It's a beautiful moment, in a beautiful place.

Released from the intensity of the search itself, I gaze around, for the first time taking in the nature of the surrounding landscape.

We are overlooking the river Don. There are wild swans and heron on the river, buzzards circle-gliding in the sky. The graveyard's surrounded by woodland which is carpeted with wild garlic. We have disturbed a sleeping deer.

I realise that I've been here before. The previous week, and many, many weeks before that.

Except the river was the Wye and the woods were the Forest of Dean.

I am suddenly very much back to where I started.

When our Diane tells me some time later that Fetternear means 'western forest' I'm not in the least surprised, I'm just excited about finding a whole new beginning for my tale.

Adult Games

Performed at the Garden Café & Gallery
May 2009

If you want to reduce stress, boost your immune system, and improve your circulation all at the same time, there is something you can do about it. Something quite delicious, that will relax muscle-tension and leave you with a warm, soft afterglow. And if you're trying to lose a bit of weight, this activity uses up to five hundred calories an hour at its peak.

Sustaining it at pitch level for an hour can, of course, be difficult. Even if, like me, you discover you have a natural bent for it, and enjoy it so much that you endeavour to practice it as regularly as you can, both in private and in public. I remember when I was fourteen peaking through an entire lesson of double-Spanish with the gorgeous and entertaining Senor Eccevaria. I might have lasted even longer but I was eventually put out of the room because the rest of the class were wanting to join in.

Yes, the value of the belly laugh cannot be denied.

Most people now know that laughter has a direct physiological effect on the body and the brain. The process of laughing, or even just smiling, floods us with feel-good endorphins, whether we're actually laughing for real or just pretending.

So why isn't there more of it about? Why do so many people say that what they could do with is a good laugh, that they just wanna have fun – and it's not just the girls?

Children laugh easily and lightly, allegedly four to six hundred times a day (who counted this?), but not adults, why is that?

For one thing, children have more opportunities for naturally-occurring fun, because children are allowed to play. There are many definitions of play, but the common agreement is that it's inherently aimless, with no need to serve any clear purpose or satisfy any intended outcome. It's doing something just for the hell of it.

For over a decade, I've been involved with a training programme for teaching assistants. Because of this, I've spent a lot of time in primary school classrooms across the Forest, Gloucester, Cheltenham, and South Wales. The nature of the learning environments varies massively from one school to another, but what they all share equally is some version of 'golden time', periods of purposeless play, offered as a reward for good behaviour, or as a release from the pressure of having to achieve.

International research has identified the importance of play as an activity that unites the mind, body and spirit; provides the opportunity to practice new skills and functions;

enables the development of curiosity, inventiveness, and persistence; provides a means of developing creative and aesthetic appreciation.

It's seen as such a valuable activity that national standards now oblige teaching assistants to prove that they can competently encourage children's creative play, can effectively play alongside to sensitively support child's play. If the TAs can't play nicely, they can't pass their qualification.

If it's such valuable behaviour, how come adults aren't doing more of it? Why are the kids having all the fun?

I'm fortunate enough that my professional work as a writer is also a great passion, and a significant source of fun. But the nature of writing is such that you often don't know if, when, how and how much you'll get paid for your work, so the lines between job and hobby are easily blurred. Some months ago I realised that everything I did, all of my so-called leisure activity, was turning purposeful.

If I read a book, I'm analysing the prose.

If I go to the theatre I'm making notes on dramatic conflict and theatrical impact.

If I go to the cinema I'm noting camera shots and sequences, holes in the plot and character arcs.

If I go for a walk, fantastical characters and their storylines are waiting round every corner, peeping out behind every tree.

If I rent a DVD I'm checking out the bonus features, tempted to skip the actual film and listen to the writer-director's commentary instead.

Even a day-trip turns into work, because I'm inspired by landscapes and settings, jotting down descriptions of my creative responses everywhere I go.

I don't resent the fact that I do what I do, because I really like the different dimensions that my writerly perceptions allow me to travel in, and they do save my sanity in traffic-jams and turn what could be a tedious five-hour wait in a hospital into a pantomime sketch.

But it does mean that doing something for the hell of it can be elusive, and has led to my cry of ... Ohmigod, I can't believe it, I've got nothing to play with, somebody's pinched me toys!

About this time I happened to be lunching in the Punch Bowl in Monmouth, when a group of chaps entered the pub together. There were about five of them, of varying age ranges, nothing remarkable about them, except for the oddity of their behaviour, because they were giggling among themselves, chuckling, laughing out loud.

Shock, horror!

Their entrance effected an immediate change of atmosphere in the pub, as if a cold wind had suddenly blown in. People began to shift uncomfortably.

These chaps weren't dressed up in corporate-away-day uniform, so this wasn't the forced jollity that can accompany such events. Nor were any of the men drunk or likely to be, the strongest drink on the table being half a lager shandy. Nor were they trying to create an effect, because they showed absolutely no awareness of anyone around them or anything other than whatever was the source of their merriment. Clearly just mates enjoying a few rounds of laughter together.

The mood of the other patrons couldn't have been more disapproving if these chaps had walked in naked. Their laughter was deemed inappropriate behaviour, it wasn't seemly.

The next morning I was at my keyboards at home when the walking bus passed along my lane heading for Lydbrook primary at the bottom of the hill. A couple of six-year-olds were accompanying their journey by singing their hearts out to Peter Kay's Amarillo, and laughing like drains whenever they came to the line where 'sweet Marie' was waiting for them. They did this right until one of the adult bus conductors shouted at them to 'stop messing about', effectively halting both the singing and laughter, stopping the fun, presumably it not being seemly.

Laughter can imply lack of control, irresponsibility, a sign of the immature and foolish. We are taught as adults to not be silly, to act our age. Fun for its own sake is discouraged the further away from childhood we travel.

It's an unnecessary loss.

There are loads of ways for us grown ups to reintroduce fun for the fun of it back into our lives.

For my part, I've bought a sweet-singing mandolin to play with, rather than to play.

I've started wearing the odd, impractical, swirly silk frock, and polishing my nails.

I've acquired oil paints and canvass with no plan but to daub.

And I've devised my own version of golden time to share with other grown-up playmates who want to give themselves a reward for good behaviour, or be released from the pressure of having to achieve.

I can't think that I'm alone in all of this, because I've recently heard about this fabulous cabaret evening where a house band creates music through pipes in a bucket and jewellery boxes, where I can join a roomful of consenting adults doing things like waving our arms in the style of Nelly the elephant's trunk, and composing our own percussion by banging two empty Vaseline tubs together. Just for the hell of it.

It doesn't seem likely, but has anybody else heard about it?

Me and Eddie

*Performed outside my back door for Charlie and Sabrina,
my neighbours' cats.
June 2009*

It's like tracing your finger along a favourite necklace, fiddling idly with the gemstones ... or like handling prayer beads ... you do it without consciously realising you're doing it, because your attention's held elsewhere.

That's how it is for me when I drive to and fro between the Forest of Dean and Sunderland, now that I've been making the journey for over twenty years.

To lose one's thread in the midst of such familiar activities would be quite unbelievable.

But like so many other unbelievable things, it's only a matter of time before it happens.

So, last autumn, I'm on a return journey back to the Forest, when, shortly before the need-to-take junction for the M18 south, I spy a middle-aged couple climbing down a grassy slope at the side of a bridge.

Where can they be going, I wonder, because there's only the motorway in front of them? And actually, where have they been, because this bridge is stuck in the middle of a wasteland, and is clearly the victim of local landscape developments that has left it all dressed up with nowhere to go.

Storyteller that I am, I spot immediately that the odd couple have created a gap where a tale should go. How lucky for them that I happened to be driving by.

I spend the next delicious driving-while making up plots and subplots for the hapless pair. Just when I've reached a satisfying climax where the murderers drop their mortal coils at the base of the bridge where their murderees are buried, something in my captive attention breaks free and registers that I'm passing a signpost for London.

Now, there are parts of my journey where the signs do include London as one of the places that lie ahead of me, but this feels a little late for the capital still to be so prominent in the signage.

I carry on driving, partly because I'm on a motorway and I legally have to, and partly because I'm still rising from the depths of bodies in a bridge. The further I drive on, the more my disquiet grows. The visual patterns that I'm passing just aren't quite right.

The unaccustomed shapes dancing on the back of my retina become increasingly insistent, until they're high-kicking on my brain's door, going 'hello in there – you do realise you're on the road less travelled, don't you? In fact never travelled, because you're lost, you do know that, don't you?'

Yes, I do.

I pull in at the next service station to consult a road map which I'm sure must be in the car somewhere, maybe in with the spare tyre. Oh yes, here it is, AA Road Atlas 1990.

Confident that I haven't particularly noticed any significant changes to the roads since 1990 … I plan a new route back, from where I am, to where I want to be. Looks like I'll have to go through Grantham, I've never been to Grantham before.

I am reminded of that old joke where a lost stranger asks a local passer-by for directions, and the local advises him 'Oh, I wouldn't start from here.'

So, I know that the journey home's going to take me hours longer than it would've done if I hadn't been ambushed by crazy killers, but I'm a bottle half-full sort of creature, so rather than spending the wayward miles grumbling to myself I choose to consider what I might be gaining by this diversion. What am I experiencing that I wouldn't have otherwise?

Not a lot really.

Persevering with the half-full concept, I realise that there's a concert of Elgar's music being broadcast on the radio, a concert that I definitely would have missed.

So, there's lots and lots of Elgar.

My only previous impressions of the lauded composer have been the in-my-humble-opinion overly pompous Pomp and Circumstance march, and a photograph picturing him as the quintessential imperialist.

I stifle a yawn. The concert's so stuffy I have to wind down the window to let in more air.

A further diversion occurs soon after – not of my own making this time, it's roadworks – determining that I never ever reach Grantham, so I'm left bottling Elgar as my only extended-trip consolation. The music drags on and on, lulling me to such an extent that it never occurs to me that I could either turn it over or off.

What feels like several days later, I arrive home.

When it is in reality several days later, I reach one of those moments when I'm seeking some brief distraction from an intense writing session, and on a whim I decide to google Elgar.

Edward Elgar was born on 2nd June 1857.

Oh!

I am beside myself.

No, really.

Me and Elgar have the same birthday, born exactly a century apart. We're virtually twins.

This new information changes everything. If we have this really-special day in common, there must be other things we share, there just must be. And not liking to miss anything, I want to know what those things are.

Maybe I've got his music all wrong, maybe I've just been listening to the bad bits.

The very next time I'm in Gloucester, I go to the Music and Drama library to seek out Elgar CDs.

The first CD I take home is Sea Pictures. This is great, I adore the sea, he must do too, why else would he compose a CD about it.

I drool over the track-titles.

Sea Slumber, which has me imagining mermaids and sirens and goddesses in upturned shells …

Sabbath Morning at Sea, which evokes a picture of lifeboats packed full of a sombre congregation who are attending silently to the pastor as he blesses the waters above the latest shipwreck.

I play the music.

It's dull. Stuffy and dull.

Disappointment is such a tedious state to be in, so I decide that I'm not in it. I must love my pseudo-twin, it's just a question of finding out exactly what it is that's loveable about him. We're mutable air signs for Mercury's sake. We are quicksilver, we fly. The Eddie-boy must have wings, and I'm going to find them if it bloody well kills me.

My ensuing explorations do throw up stuff we have in common. Elgar was an early riser. Me too. His mam was called Anne, his dad was called William. Mine too. He attended, odd as it seems, an all girls' Catholic school, and so did I ... although for him it was as a six-year-old and because his sisters went there, and for me it was at sixteen because St Anthony's Convent School was where all the Catholic girls in Sunderland went to do their A levels.

So far, so bizarre.

But this is the mundane and earth-bound, I want more. What about his inspirations, his passions, his creative processes.

I dig a little deeper.

I discover a treasure trove of textbooks about him in Ross-on-Wye library, and read one after another after another.

I blow a generous HMV gift voucher on yet more Elgarian music, this time in box sets – unexpectedly fitting I realise when I read that Elgar opened the very first HMV shop in London in 1921.

Back to 2009, I begin to work my way through the music systematically, testing each track for mercurial potential.

I'm just beginning to consider the nightmare possibility that I might actually be wrong, when, sat reading in the sunshine outside my French windows on a May Bank Holiday, stereo on low in the background, I am suddenly captivated.

Hello, hello, hello, I wonder, what's that?

Whatever it is I love it.

I look up the track on the CD cover.

Serenade! From the Wand of Youth, a musical play that he wrote with his brothers and sisters when he was twelve, a magical tale set in a forested glade that is intersected by a stream with the material world on one side, the ephereal on the other.

This is more up my flight path.

I listen on ...

... to the sun and fountain dance ...

... to moths and butterflies ...

... to wild and tame bears ...

... to the Nursery Suite with its sad and merry and serious dolls.

I follow little bells and mystical pipers to a land of giants and dream children and slumber.

At last! I have found my bridge to Elgar, in fairy-land no less.

I learn that Elgar's surname means elf-spear ... the elfin flood-gates pour open.

I join the Elgar society.

I visit his Broadheath birthplace museum.

I wander, as he wandered, in Spetchley Park.

I learn that he has a wicked sense of humour and a love of mystery ... I delight in the discovery that he wrote in the ancient Ogham script, a runic language I've only just become aware of myself.

And without the prejudice of thinking he's a stuffed-shirt conventionalist, I'm listening to his music with a fresh ear, and liking it.

He's become my new muse.

He's inspiring me with his Caractacan tale of druids and woodlands, and with his Gerontian dream of heaven and earth.

His Apostles are tempting me to write my own mystery plays.

His Severn Suite is swelling my explorations into riversides.

And I'm liking enormously the notion behind his Enigma Variations – musical portraits of his family and friends. I might very well have a little twiddle with this myself. Perhaps my friends and family members should be warned.

Me and Eddie, now the greatest of mates.

All because I missed the turn off for the M18, all because of an odd couple on a bridge.

I must go back and find out what's been waiting for me in Grantham.

From Wear to Wye

*Performed at the Kavern Bar, Angel Hotel, Coleford
and the Old Station, Tintern
July 2009*

I am a saltwater girl, born in Sunderland, within tidal distance of the sea.

I am fluvian, born in Southwick, Sunderland, a village that lies on the banks of the river that feeds into that sea.

The River Wear rises in the Pennines and travels east, passing my used-to-be-home shortly before it flows between two piers and out into the North Sea.

So for me there was always the river ... perpetually passing by ... but at the same time, perpetually still there, exactly where it always had been.

Clever!

To stay where you are and simultaneously move on is a bit like having your cake and eating it. Although I've never been that fussed about cake, the ability to be in two places at the same time is something I've always wanted to do, perpetually.

The behaviour of rivers and the impact of their movements make for an interesting study.

As a river journeys it continuously gathers up, sets back down, gathers up, sets back down along the way. These fluvial gatherings include physical matter of course – small stones, sand, and scraps of vegetation – but that's not all of it.

Because part of the make up of a river includes rain that has fallen through an atmosphere filled with the sounds and scents of the localities it passes through. And part includes water that has seeped from the lands along its banks, with all of their human activities.

What comes down a river are echoes and whisperings, fragments and detachments of the lives being lived along its watercourse.

The Wear was a constant invitation to me to go off and explore those echoes and whisperings, experience something of those lives for myself

The alluring Wear, full of nuance and suggestion.

Its suggestive behaviour grew bolder and bolder towards me as the years went by.

A river has the energy to move rocks; with what little ease can it tug at the spirit of a child … a girl … a young woman.

I am twenty-three. Perpetually curious, I have indulged an overwhelming desire to learn things, and an emerging desire to share those things, by taking a teaching degree.

Now it's time to go forth and share – starting with the year tens in Tenterden High School.

With a hop, skip and a jump I'm in Kent.

Folkestone beach, ferries into France, Canterbury Cathedral and Woodchurch Windmill. The Ashford markets. Oast houses and hopfields, and games of bat 'n trap at the Six Bells Inn.

Kent.

For three years.

And then I'm restless.

Perpetually curious, with a hop, skip and a jump I'm in Essex.

Arched bridges and a Christmas circus in Central Park, only a half- hour ride on the train to London. Covent Garden street theatre and the stalls at Camden Lock, Notting Hill parades and a terraced house in Station Road, Braintree, facing the all-singing, all-drinking Sean O'Malley's pub.

Essex.

For three years.

And then I'm restless

I have noted the trinity trend, and, while I'm willing to accept this as part of my likely mercurial destiny, I decide that this time I want to have a good lookie at the map first before I leap.

I spread Britain out across the kitchen floor, and start reviewing the situation.

June-baby that I am, I'd like to stay in the embrace of the warmth that I've grown accustomed to. South then.

And everywhere I've been up to now has been east. So it's obviously time to go west.

So I'm looking for a south-westerly.

And perhaps I'm missing the cliffs or something, but I'm fed up with flatlands and the monotony of their terrain, so somewhere hilly would be ideal.

I stick pins in appropriate areas of the south-west, wander down to the market place – which for me at the time is the Times Educational Supplement – and begin the quest for my further fortune.

It's not long before I'm offered an interview at a college in Cinderford, which is in somewhere called the Forest of Dean.

The interview's first thing on a Friday morning so I decide to arrive the night before and stay over, but because repeated requests for where-to-stay information have been ignored, I turn up in the Forest with no place to stay. This doesn't concern me. How hard can it be to find a resting place, I think to myself, not comprehending the significance of a coinciding rugby game that has swallowed up every last morsel of hotel and bed-and-breakfast.

I've resigned myself to sleeping in the car when, deep into Littledean, a ghostly looking hamlet if ever I saw one, there appears an inviting driveway. I accept the invitation and soon discover that I've stumbled across a family-run, just-taken-over, not-ready-to-open-yet hotel that does, however, have a solitary finished room that could be rented out to me at a push. I provide the push and am taken in.

The whole place is in relative debris, but the finished bedroom is swish, with gold dolphins in the en suite.

The evening is surreal, because the family includes an ancient grandmother who plays a grand piano all night, a chattering parrot on a perch, and a nine year old boy who chain-crunches packet after packet of smoky bacon crisps and, unchallenged, drops every empty packet on the floor.

I can't remember hearing anything in the river's echoes that might have led me to expect any of this.

Nor the surprise result of the all-day interview at the college (surprise, because among the six of us at the interview I sure as hell wouldn't single me out for the job).

Nor the camping adventures that are to accompany finding a new Forest home, nor moving house during Hurricane Mary, nor the brace of babies I am unwittingly carrying, nor the summer spent on a cottage roof reading French.

Nor many, many other happenings that fall outside the scope of this sketch and must wait to be the subjects of other tales.

Suffice to say that I'm confident from the outset that this is going to be a wicked place to spend three years.

There were so many things I hadn't made sense of back then; so many things I didn't understand.

It's only this year, when I am twenty-three years in the Forest, that certain realisations have begun to dawn.

Like the fact that I've actually been following rivers ever since I left the north-east.

Like the knowledge that I've been gathering up and setting back down from the Wear to the Stour, from the Chelmer to the Blackwater to here.

I am fluvian, living in Lydbrook, a village that lies on the banks of the River Wye.

I am fluvian, travelling to and fro along a watercourse, and staying where I am, all at the same time.